Vegan Desserts

50 Delicious Recipes For Vegan Beginners

FREE DOWNLOAD

THE QUICKEST WAY TO GET IN SHAPE AS A VEGAN...

Table of Contents

Introduction

Let's do a headcount first! If you are sitting in a room full of people, ask them to raise their hand if they like desserts.

You would notice that almost everyone around you will raise their hands sky high and start giving you a sweet smile in hopes that you will provide them with a dessert at that very moment!

This is exactly the magic of a dessert.

Everyone always looks forward to one after a hearty meal. They are your showstoppers and the means of bringing a day full of hardship to a happy ending.

But here's the thing, people who are new to veganism often believe that being vegan spells the end of eating tasty desserts! Well, I am here to prove them wrong and provide you with a lot of wonderful recipes to show that you can enjoy a life full of mind-blowing desserts as a vegan!

But before I let you in on the recipes, let me talk just a little bit about the vegan diet itself, as to ensure that anyone (even a non-vegan) is easily able to jump into the diet with the help of this book!

If you have picked up or downloaded this book, then I am sure you also plan on following the same vegan path that many others have followed as well.

If that is the case, then I assure you that you going to the find the information and recipes in this book to be extremely helpful and you'll love what you create!

this document, including, but not limited to, —errors, omissions, or inaccuracies.

Chapter 1

Getting to Know the Vegan Diet

What Does a Vegan Diet Mean?

Speaking in the simplest of terms, being vegan is a form of diet where a person is to avoid every kind of products that are based (either directly or indirectly) on animals.

This means that meat is completely off the table as well as animal derived products such as milk and cheese.

If you ever get the privilege of asking devoted vegan followers as to "why" they are doing this. You might expect an answer such as, "I want to be healthy". Which would be correct in most cases, but for the most die-hard devotees, veganism is not only a way of eating, but rather it is a definition of how they carry out their life. In fact, the vegan lifestyle is often considered to be a revolution against animal cruelty and exploitation.

It should be noted that there is a fine difference between vegetarianism and veganism, so the two are not to be confused. Individuals who follow a vegan diet tend to completely restrict themselves from having any kind of dairy/animal products as mentioned above. However, vegetarians have a certain level of freedom in this department that allows them to have certain animal derived products such as eggs or cheese.

The dessert recipes found in this book are written with for vegans in mind, so, they are super compatible with a vegetarian diet as well.

The Different Types of Vegan Diet

Now that you know the basic guidelines for a vegan diet, you should know that there are actual different types of vegan diets.

Some of the most popular ones are described below.

- **Whole food Vegan Diet:** This diet emphasizes different kinds of whole plant foods such as nuts, seeds, legumes, fruits, whole grains etc.
- **Raw-Food Vegan Diet:** This diet is composed of nuts, raw fruits, plant foods, vegetables, seeds that are cooked under a temperature of 118 degrees Fahrenheit.
- **80/10/10:** This unique diet encourages an individual to rely on fat rich plants such as avocados and nuts and focuses more on raw fruits and tender greens. This diet is also known as "the fruitarian diet".
- **The Starch Solution:** This is like the fruitarian diet with the exception that it focuses on cooked starches such as rice, potatoes, and corn instead of raw fruits.
- **Raw Till 4:** This is a low-fat diet that is a variation of the fruitarian and starch solution diets. In this diet, raw fruits are consumed up until 4 PM, after which, the individual has the option to cook a nice plant based meal to end the day with.
- **Junk Food Vegan Diet:** This diet relies largely on mock meats and vegan compliant cheese, desserts and fries. Not to mention, other heavily processed vegan produces as well!

These variations allow different types of people to easily pick the diet that suits them the most according to their health condition or dietary preference.

I encourage you to play around with some to find one that suits you best. Although it should be noted that not all diets are created equal!

A junk food vegan diet will not be as beneficial for you health as say a whole food vegan diet.

Chapter 2

General Rules of the Diet

With the fundamentals of the diet out of the way, here we will be discussing a bit about the staple guidelines as to how you can follow the diet.

A general guideline on the diet

If you are completely new to this diet and just want to give it a whirl, instead of exploring all those different diet variations, simply keep the following points in mind.

- Try to eat at least five portions of veggies and fruits with loads of varieties throughout the day.
- Make sure to keep your base meals circled around rice, bread, potatoes, pasta and other starchy carbs.
- Go for dairy alternatives such as soya drinks, almond milk and other low fat/low sugar options.
- Try to pack in some spirulina and beans to ensure that you are supplied with protein.
- If using oil and spreads, make sure to go for unsaturated ones and in small portions.
- Make sure to keep yourself packed with lots of fluid, preferably 6-8 cups of water per day.

Allowed Foods

These are the foods that should always be on your list when you go to the store.

- **Tofu, Seitan, and Tempeh:** These are excellent providers of proteins and are rich alternatives to fish, poultry and meat.
- **Legumes:** These include beans, peas, and lentils. They are also great sources of many essential nutrients and beneficial plant compounds.
- **Nuts and Nut Butters:** Go for pure unroasted and unblanched ones as they are packed with selenium, zinc, fiber, iron etc.
- **Seeds:** Flaxseed, hemp, and chia are good choices when it comes to seeds as they are packed with a good dose of omega-3 fatty acids and protein.
- **Algae:** Chlorella and Spirulina are good choices when it comes to seeking out good sources of protein packed Algae.
- **Calcium Fortified Plant Milks:** These are excellent alternatives for a vegan to meet their daily recommended dietary calcium intake.
- **Nutritional Yeast:** This is yet another means of easily obtaining a large amount of protein from Vegan meals. Make sure to go for the ones that are labeled "Vitamin B12" fortified for maximum benefit.
- **Sprouted and Fermented Plant Foods:** Products such as tempeh, natto, miso, pickles, kombucha, and Kimchi fall under this category and they offer a good amount of vitamin K2 and probiotics.
- **Whole Grain Cereals and Pseudocereals:** These are good providers of complex carbs, iron and Vitamin B.
- **Vegetables and Fruits:** These should make up the bulk of your diet. They are amazing sources of nutrients and leafy

greens including bok Choy, kale, mustard greens and even spinach are jam packed with calcium and iron.

Restricted Foods

As a vegan, you need to avoid these foods at all costs. Some are easy to miss but others can be hard to spot, make it a habit to read product labels whenever you are buying something you're unsure about.

- **Meat:** Lamb, beef, veal, chicken, turkey, quail, duck, etc.
- **Fish and Seafood:** All types of sea food are restricted including squid, shrimp, anchovies, calamari, crab etc.
- **Eggs:** Any kind of eggs, including ostrich, quail, chicken, and fish are off the table.
- **Dairy:** Ice Cream, cheese, cream, milk, butter are restricted.
- **Animal Based Products and Ingredients:** Whey, lactose, casein, egg white albumen, carmine, gelatin etc. are to be avoided.
- **Bee Products:** Royal jelly, pollen, honey etc. are to be avoided as well.

If you are new to the diet, then the list above might discourage a little bit as you are essentially sacrificing a lot here. However, rest assure that the advantages of the diet are far greater than the sacrifices that are made, as you will see in the next chapter.

Chapter 3

Understanding the Advantages and Risks Associated with Veganism

Up until now I have just discussed the basic concepts of the diet, now let's have a look at the reasons as to "why" you should try to follow a vegan diet in the first place!

Amazing advantages of being a Vegan

- Protection from various chronic diseases such as Type 2 Diabetes
- Greatly reduce the possibility of you suffering from Cardiovascular diseases or Ischemic heart diseases
- Relieve your stress and keep you free from hypertension
- Lower the possibility of you suffering from a stroke
- Help you prevent obesity
- Protection against various cancers, including colon and prostate
- Increase the health of your bones, and your kidney functionality
- Help prevent the development of Alzheimer's

Those are just the tip of the ice berg!

Most people start to feel better just a few weeks into a vegan diet. If you are eating healthy foods and performing some form of exercise frequently then your body will thank you!

Some risks to keep in mind

Many common risks associated with the diet come from years of eating an omnivorous diet. Therefore, there are certain vitamins and minerals that are difficult to obtain when solely relying on vegetable and fruits alone.

It is highly recommended that you prepare a well-defined vegan plan before going into the diet, otherwise your body might suffer from certain vitamin and mineral deficiencies.

However, it should be noted that overcoming these deficiencies is pretty easy, so there's nothing to worry about in the long run!

The ones that you should keep in mind include Vitamin B12, Omega 3, Iron, Zinc, Iodine and Calcium deficiencies.

And to tackle them, you should:

- Make sure to included foods that are fortified with calcium, vitamin B12 and Vitamin D on your plate. Examples include fortified almond or rice milk, soy, orange juice, collard greens, turnips, bok Choy, dried figs etc.
- Try to ferment sprouts and cook your food in order to enhance absorption of zinc and iron
- Make sure to use iron cast pots and pans while cooking and avoid drinking coffee or tea with iron rich foods
- A little bit of iodized salt or seaweed will help maintain appropriate iodine levels
- For long chain Omega-3's, go for chia, flaxseeds, soybeans, hemp etc.

And just in case you are wondering, yes! Vegans are allowed to take supplements. In fact it is actually recommended that you take the appropriate supplements should you face any troubles.

But make sure to consult with your physician first.

Common Supplements to keep in mind and how to take them are listed below.

- **Vitamin B12:** Try to take supplements that contain B12 in cyanocobalamin form for maximum effectiveness.
- **Vitamin D:** Go for D2 or Vegan D3.
- **EPA and DHA:** Take from algae oil.
- **Iron:** Should only be ingested as a supplement if you have a severe deficiency. Otherwise, avoid taking extra Iron.
- **Iodine:** Either take supplements or add 1/2 a teaspoon of iodized salt to your daily diet.
- **Calcium:** Take tablets of 500mg or less daily, make sure to test your levels first.
- **Zinc:** Take in forms of Zinc Citrate or Zinc Gluconate.

With that said, you are now ready to explore the amazing desserts of the Vegan world!

Chapter 4

50 Dessert Recipes

1 Easy Granola Skillet

Prep Time: 7 minutes
Cooking Time: 12 minutes
Serving size: 3

Ingredients

- 5 pitted Medjool dates
- 1/4 cup of boiling water
- 1 tablespoon of coconut oil (melted)
- 1 tablespoon of cinnamon
- 1/4 teaspoon of sea salt
- 2 cups of rolled oats
- 1 cup of raw nuts

Cooking Directions

1. Take a food processor and add in the water, dates, cinnamon, oil, and salt. Puree the whole mixture until it is smooth.
2. Transfer it to a large sized bowl and stir in your oats, seeds, and nuts
3. Take a 12-inch skillet and place it over medium heat
4. Add the mixture and cook for about 12 minutes, make sure to keep stirring it regularly
5. Let it cool and serve!

Nutritional Values

- Calories: 140
- Fat: 6g
- Carbohydrates: 17g

- Protein: 2.5g

2 Feisty Chia and Oatmeal Cookies

Serving: 4
Prep Time: 15 minutes
Cook Time: 10 minutes

Ingredients

- 2 cups of rolled oatmeal
- 1 cup of brown sugar
- 2/3 cup of whole wheat flour
- 3 tablespoons of chia seeds
- 1 teaspoon of ground cinnamon
- 1 teaspoon of baking soda
- 1/2 a teaspoon of baking powder
- 1/2 a teaspoon of salt
- 2/3 cup of applesauce
- 2 and 1/2 tablespoons of coconut oil
- 1 cup of dried cranberries
- 1/2 a cup of dark chocolate chips
- 1/4 cup of shredded, unsweetened coconut

Cooking Directions

1. Pre-heat your oven to 350 degrees Fahrenheit
2. Next, prepare a baking sheet by lining it with parchment paper
3. Take a bowl and add the oats, flour, sugar, chia seeds, baking soda, cinnamon, baking powder, and salt
4. Mix well
5. Stir in your applesauce alongside coconut oil into the oat mix and keep mixing until you have an even dough

6. Throw in chocolate chips (if using), cranberries and coconut
7. Spoon the dough onto your baking sheet
8. Bake for 10-15 minutes and enjoy!

Nutritional Values

- Calories: 262
- Fats: 8g
- Carbs:47g
- Protein:3.4g

3 Traditional Vegan Orange Cake

Serving: 4
Prep Time: 15 minutes
Cook Time: 30 minutes

Ingredients

- 1 large sized peeled orange
- 1 and a 1/2 cup of all-purpose flour
- 1 cup of white sugar
- 1/2 a cup of vegetable oil
- 1 and 1/2 teaspoon of baking soda
- 1/2 teaspoon of salt

Cooking Directions

1. Pre-heat your oven to 375 degrees Fahrenheit
2. Take an 8x8 inch baking pan and grease it well
3. Next, take a blender and blend the orange, make sure you get at least 1 cup of orange juice
4. Take a bowl and whisk in orange juice, vegetable oil, sugar, baking soda, and salt
5. Mix well and pour the prepared batter into your pan
6. Bake for about 30 minutes until a toothpick comes out clean from the center
7. Enjoy!

Nutritional Values

- Calories: 145
- Fats: 8g
- Carbs:20g
- Protein:1.3g

 **4**

Ravishing Choco-Nut Banana Bites

Serving: 4
Preparation Time: 10 minutes
Cook Time: 0 minute

Ingredients

- 5 teaspoons of cocoa powder
- 4 teaspoons of toasted unsweetened coconut
- 2 sliced up small bananas

Cooking Directions

1. Take two individual plates and place the cocoa and coconut on those plates (individually)
2. Roll up the banana slices in the cocoa first and shake off any excess
3. Then dip them in the coconut
4. Serve!

Nutritional Values

- Calories: 55
- Fats: 1g
- Carbs: 14g
- Protein: 1g

5   Merry Melon Soup

Serving: 4
Prep Time: 15 minutes
Cook Time: 0 minutes

Ingredients

- 5 cups of casaba melon, cubed and seeded
- 3/4 cups of coconut milk
- Juice from 2 limes
- 1 tablespoon of freshly grated ginger
- 1 pinch of salt

Cooking Directions

1. Add the coconut milk, casaba melon, lime juice, salt, and ginger to your food processor
2. Process it for about 1-2 minutes until the mixture has a soup like texture
3. Enjoy!

Nutritional Values

- Calories: 120
- Fats: 9g
- Carbs:10g
- Protein:2g

 # Fantastic Vegan Butter Balls with Almonds

Serving: 4
Prep Time: 10 minutes
Cook Time: 0 minutes

Ingredients

- 11 pieces of diced and pitted dates
- 1/3 cup of unsweetened shredded coconut
- 2 and a 1/2 tablespoon of almond butter

Cooking Directions

1. Take a bowl and add dates, almond butter, and coconut
2. Mix well
3. Use the mixture to form small balls
4. Store them in your fridge and chill them overnight
5. Enjoy!

Nutritional Values

- Calories: 60
- Fats: 3g
- Carbs:7g
- Protein:1g

7 Tapioca Strawberry Mix

Serving: 4
Prep Time: 15 minutes
Cook Time: 0 minutes

Ingredients

- 1 cup of fresh strawberries, halved and hulled
- 1 and a 1/2 cup of water
- 1/4 cup of quick-cooking tapioca

Cooking Directions

1. Take your blender, add the berries and water
2. Process for a few minutes until a smooth mixture forms
3. Add the tapioca and allow it to sit for about 10 minutes
4. Bring the mixture to a boil over medium heat, making sure to keep stirring it from time to time
5. Pour the mix into serving dishes and enjoy!

Nutritional Values

- Calories: 50
- Fats: 7g
- Carbs:13g
- Protein:2g

8 The Original Vegan Gelatin

Serving: 4
Prep Time: 4 hours 10 minutes
Cook Time: 0 minutes

- 1/2 a teaspoon of cornstarch
- 1 and 1/2 teaspoons of water
- 2 cups of cherry juice
- 1 teaspoon of agar-agar

Cooking Directions

1. Take a small cup and dissolve the cornstarch
2. Keep the bowl on the side
3. Take a saucepan and add 1 and a 1/2 cups of cherry juice alongside the agar-agar powder
4. Allow the mixture to sit for about 5 minutes
5. After 5 minutes, set it over medium-high heat and simmer for about 1 minute
6. Remove the heat and stir in the remaining juice alongside cornstarch mix
7. Pour the mixture into small cups and chill the for about 4 hours
8. Serve and enjoy!

Nutritional Values

- Calories: 25
- Fats: 0g
- Carbs: 4g
- Protein: 0g

9 Healthy Almond Melon Salad

Serving: 4
Prep Time: 15 minutes
Cook Time: 0 minutes

- 2 tablespoons of fresh lime juice
- 1 teaspoon of white sugar
- 1 teaspoon of minced fresh ginger root
- 1/4 cup of vegetable oil
- 2 bunch of chopped up and trimmed watercress
- 2 and a 1/2 cups of cubed watermelon
- 2 and a 1/2 cups of cubed cantaloupe
- 1/3 cup of toasted and sliced almonds

Cooking Directions

1. Take a large sized bowl and add sugar, lime juice, and ginger
2. Whisk well and add oil
3. Season with some pepper and salt
4. Add watercress, cantaloupe, and watermelon
5. Toss well to coat it up
6. Transfer the mix to salad bowls
7. Garnish a with a bit of sliced almonds and enjoy!

Nutrition Values

- Calories: 257
- Fats: 18g
- Carbs: 21g
- Protein: 9g

10   Simple Vegan Truffle

Serving: 4
Prep Time: 20 minutes
Cook Time: 10 minutes

- 1 and a 1/2 cup of shredded unsweetened coconut
- 2 cups of Mejdool dates
- 1 cup of raw almonds
- 2 and a 1/4 cup of raw cocoa powder
- 1/2 a cup of cocoa nibs
- 1/2 a cup of agave nectar
- 2 teaspoons of vanilla extract
- 1 teaspoon of salt

Cooking Directions

1. Pre-heat your oven to 350 degrees Fahrenheit
2. Spread out the coconut on a baking sheet
3. Line another baking sheet with parchment paper
4. Bake the coconut in your oven for about 7 minutes, making sure to keep stirring them from time to time
5. Take a food processor, add in dates and almonds then process until smooth
6. Add cocoa powder and process until mixed well
7. Transfer mix to a bowl
8. Add in 1 cup of your toasted coconut, agave nectar, salt and vanilla extract into the date mix. Mix well
9. Roll up the dough into tablespoon sized balls and roll them in the remaining toasted truffle balls.

10. Transfer the balls to your parchment lined baking sheet and allow them to harden for about 60 minutes
11. Enjoy!

Nutritional Values

- Calories: 26
- Fats: 0g
- Carbs: 6g
- Protein: 0g

11 Guilt and Dairy-Free Chocolate Pudding

Serving: 4
Prep Time: 10 minutes
Cook Time: 10 minutes

Ingredients

- 3 tablespoons of cornstarch
- 2 and 1/2 tablespoons of water
- 1 and a 1/2 cups of soy milk
- 1/4 teaspoon of vanilla extract
- 1/4 cup of white sugar
- 1/4 cup of unsweetened cocoa powder

Cooking Directions

1. Take a small sized bowl and add cornstarch and water then mix well to form a nice paste like texture
2. Take a large sized saucepan and place it over medium heat
3. Add soy milk, sugar, vanilla, cocoa and your prepared cornstarch mixture
4. Give the whole mixture a stir and allow it to cook until boiling point is reached
5. Keep stirring until the mixture is thick
6. Remove the heat
7. Allow it to cool and chill in your fridge until it is fully cooled and has settled in
8. Enjoy!

Nutritional Values

- Calories: 256
- Fats: 5g
- Carbs:52g
- Protein:9.5g

12   Subtle Cherry Crisp

Serving: 4
Prep Time: 10 minutes
Cook Time: 30 minutes

Ingredients

- 21-ounce cherry pie filling
- 1/2 a cup of all-purpose flour
- 1/2 a cup of rolled oats
- 2/3 cup of brown sugar
- 1 teaspoon of ground cinnamon
- 3/4 teaspoon of ground nutmeg
- 1/4 cup of chopped up pecans
- 1/3 cup of vegan butter

Cooking Directions

1. Pre-heat your oven to 350 degrees Fahrenheit
2. Take a 2-quart baking dish and grease it up
3. Pour the pie filling mixture evenly into the dish and spread it up
4. Take a medium sized bowl and add flour, sugar, oats, cinnamon and nutmeg
5. Add melted margarine and mix, spread this mixture over your pie filling
6. Sprinkle chopped up pecans
7. Bake for 30 minutes until the top shows a golden brown texture
8. Allow it to cool for about 15 minutes and enjoy!

Nutritional Values

- Calories: 345
- Fats: 14g
- Carbs:55g
- Protein:3g

13 Sugary Tortilla Strips

Serving: 4
Prep Time: 10 minutes
Cook Time: 1 minutes

Ingredients

- 1 and 1/2 cups of white sugar
- 1 teaspoon of ground cinnamon
- 11/4 teaspoon of ground nutmeg
- 10 pieces of 8 inch flour tortillas
- 3 cups of oil

Cooking Directions

1. Take a re-sealable bag and add nutmeg, cinnamon, and sugar
2. Mix well and toss
3. Take a deep skillet and add oil
4. Heat the oil up to 375 degrees Fahrenheit and fry 4-5 tortilla strips for about 30 seconds until browned
5. Transfer the strips to the re-sealable bag and toss them well to coat the strips with the sugary mix
6. Serve or store in containers and serve later

Nutritional Values

- Calories: 85
- Fats: 2.8g
- Carbs:14g
- Protein:1.4g

14 Hearty Banana Cookies

Serving: 4
Prep Time: 15 minutes
Cook Time: 20 minutes

Ingredients

- 4 ripe bananas
- 2 cups of rolled up oats
- 1 cup of dates, chopped up and pitted
- 1/3 cup of vegetable oil
- 1 teaspoon of vanilla extract

Cooking Directions

1. Pre-heat your oven to 350 degrees Fahrenheit
2. Take a large sized bowl and add bananas
3. Mash them well and add oats, oil, dates and vanilla
4. Mix well and allow the mixture to sit for 15 minutes
5. Drop little circles of the mixture onto an ungreased cookie sheet
6. Bake for about 20 minutes in your oven until each cookies shows a light brown texture
7. Enjoy!

Nutritional Values

- Calories: 58
- Fats: 2.5g
- Carbs:9g
- Protein:1g

15 Balsamic Glazed Strawberries

Serving: 4
Prep Time: 70 minutes
Cook Time: 0 minutes

Ingredients

- 18 ounces of fresh strawberries, hulled with the large berries cut up in half
- 2 tablespoons of balsamic vinegar
- 1/2 cup of white sugar
- 1/4 teaspoon of fresh ground black pepper

Cooking Directions

1. Take a bowl and add the strawberries
2. Drizzle vinegar over your berries and sprinkle a bit of sugar
3. Stir well
4. Cover and allow it to sit at room temp for at least 1 hour and max 4 hours
5. Serve with a grind of pepper
6. Enjoy!

Nutritional Values

- Calories: 60
- Fats: 0.3g
- Carbs: 14g
- Protein:0.5g

16 Gentle As A Breeze Quinoa Pudding

Serving: 5
Prep Time: 5 minutes
Cook Time: 35 minutes

Ingredients

- 1 cup of quinoa
- 2 cups of water
- 2 cups of apple juice
- 1 and 1/2 cups of raisins
- 2 tablespoon of lemon juice
- 1 teaspoon of ground cinnamon
- Salt as needed
- Pepper as needed
- 2 teaspoons of vanilla extract

Cooking Directions

1. Gently add the quinoa in a sieve and rinse it well
2. Drain them
3. Add the quinoa to a medium sized saucepan and add water
4. Bring it to a boil and cover with a lid, then lower the lid down a bit and simmer until the quinoa has absorbed the water and are tender
5. Add apple juice, lemon juice, raisins and salt
6. Cover it up with a pan and allow it to simmer for 15 minutes
7. Stir in vanilla extract and serve warm to enjoy!

Nutritional Values

- Calories: 200
- Fats: 2g
- Carbs:40g
- Protein:7g

17   Beautiful Eggless Brownies

Serving: 6
Prep Time: 20 minutes
Cook Time: 25 minutes

Ingredients

- 1/3 cup of all-purpose flour
- 1 cup of water
- 1/2 a cup of vegan butter
- 1 cup of unsweetened cocoa powder
- 2 cups of white sugar
- 1 teaspoon of vanilla extract
- 2 cups of all-purpose flour
- 2 and a 1/2 teaspoons of baking powder
- 1/2 a teaspoon of salt
- 1/2 a cup of chopped up walnuts

Cooking Directions

1. Pre-heat your oven to 350 degrees Fahrenheit
2. Take a 9x13 inch pan and grease it up
3. Take a heavy saucepan and add 1/3 cup of flour and water
4. Cook over medium heat, making sure to keep stirring in well until you have a thick mixture
5. Transfer to a mixing bowl and keep it on the side
6. Take a small sized saucepan and melt your vegan butter
7. Once the butter has melted enough, add cocoa and mix well
8. Allow it to stand and cool
9. Beat the vanilla and sugar to your cooled flour mix

10. Stir in cocoa mix and keep stirring until blended well
11. Add flour, salt and baking powder and stir well until the batter has blended
12. Fold in some walnuts and spread the mixture evenly in your pan
13. Bake for 20-25 minutes until a toothpick comes out clean from the center
14. Enjoy!

Nutritional Values

- Calories: 200
- Fats: 7g
- Carbs:32g
- Protein:2.6g

18 Children's Special Oatmeal Cookie

Serving: 4
Prep Time: 5 minutes
Cook Time: 3 minutes

Ingredients

- 1 cup of maple syrup
- 1/4 cup of vegetable oil
- 5 tablespoon of unsweetened cocoa powder
- 1 teaspoon of ground cinnamon
- 1/2 a cup of peanut butter
- 1 cup of rolled oats
- 1 teaspoon of vanilla extract

Cooking Directions

1. Take a saucepan and place it over medium heat
2. Add maple syrup, cocoa, oil, cinnamon and boil for about 3 minutes, making sure to keep stirring it from time to time
3. Remove your heat and stir in peanut butter, vanilla and rolled oats
4. Take spoonfuls of the mixture and dollop them onto a waxed paper
5. Allow them to chill for 30 minutes
6. Enjoy!

Nutrition Values

- Calories: 91
- Fats: 8g

- Carbs: 9g
- Protein: 3g

19   **Sweet Candied Apples**

Serving: 4
Prep Time: 10 minutes
Cook Time: 30 minutes

Ingredients

- 15-20 apples
- 2 and 1/2 cups of white sugar
- 1 cup of light corn syrup
- 1 and a 1/2 cup of water
- 8 drops of red food coloring

Cooking Directions

1. Lightly grease up your cookie sheets
2. Insert craft sticks into your stemmed apples
3. Take a medium sized saucepan and place it over medium-high heat
4. Add sugar, water and corn syrup and heat it up until the temperature reaches 300 degrees Fahrenheit
5. Remove the heat and stir in food coloring
6. Take the apples and hold them by the stick, dip them in syrup and coat them evenly
7. Transfer them on a wax sheet and allow to harden
8. Enjoy!

Nutritional Values

- Calories: 240
- Fats: 1g

- Carbs: 62g
- Protein: 0.4g

20 Hefty Vegan Banana Brownies

Serving: 4
Prep Time: 15 minutes
Cook Time: 25 minutes

Ingredients

- 2 cups of unbleached all-purpose flour
- 2 cups of white sugar
- 3 ripe bananas
- 1 cup of unsweetened cocoa powder
- 1 teaspoon of baking powder
- 1 teaspoon of salt
- 1 cup of water
- 1 cup of vegetable oil
- 1 teaspoon of vanilla extract

Cooking Directions

1. Pre-heat your oven to 350 degrees Fahrenheit
2. Take a large sized bowl and add flour, cocoa powder, banana, sugar, baking powder and salt
3. Give it a nice stir and mix well
4. Spread the mixture evenly into a 9x13 inch baking pan
5. Bake for about 25-30 minutes until the top no longer shows a "shiny" texture
6. Allow it to cool for 10 minutes
7. Enjoy!

Nutritional Values

- Calories: 290
- Fats: 14g
- Carbs: 40g
- Protein:2.4g

21 Simplified Tofu Pumpkin Pie

Serving: 6
Prep Time: 5 minutes
Cook Time: 55 minutes

Ingredients

- 10 and a 1/2 ounce of packed silken tofu (drained up)
- 16 ounces of pumpkin puree
- 1 cup of white sugar
- 1/2 a teaspoon of salt
- 1 teaspoon of ground cinnamon
- 1/2 a teaspoon of ground ginger
- 1/4 teaspoon of ground cloves
- 1 piece of 9-inch unbaked pie crust (make sure it's vegan compatible)

Cooking Directions

1. Pre-heat your oven to 450 degrees Fahrenheit
2. Take a blender and add tofu, sugar, pumpkin, salt, ginger and cloves and blend them well until you have a smooth mix
3. Pour the mixture into your pie crust and mix well
4. Bake in your oven for 15 minutes and lower down the heat to 350 degrees Fahrenheit
5. Keep baking until a knife comes out clean (should take around 40 minutes)
6. Enjoy once ready!

Nutritional Values

- Calories: 245
- Fats: 9g
- Carbs: 34g
- Protein: 4.6g

22 Finely Candied Orange and Lemon Peel

Serving: 4
Prep Time: 10 minutes
Cook Time: 30 minutes

Ingredients

- 6 pieces of lemon peels, cut up into 1/4-inch strips
- 6 pieces of orange peels cut up into 1/4-inche strips
- 2 cups of white sugar
- 1 cup of water
- 1/3 cup of white sugar

Cooking Directions

1. Take a large sized saucepan and place the lemon and orange peels on the pan
2. Bring the water to a boil over high heat
3. Keep boiling for 20 minutes
4. Drain them and keep them on the side
5. Take a medium sized saucepan and add 2 cups of sugar and 1 cup of water
6. Bring it to a boil and keep cooking until the mixture shows a thread like texture with a temperature of 230 degrees Fahrenheit
7. Stir in the peels and simmer for 5 minutes
8. Drain them and roll up the peels (not altogether) in sugar and allow them to dry
9. Enjoy!

Nutritional Values

- Calories: 165
- Fats: 0g
- Carbs: 40g
- Protein: 0.1g

23 Authentic Vegan Rose Meringues

Serving: 6
Prep Time: 30 minutes
Cook Time: 90 minutes

Ingredients

- 3/4 cup of chickpea water
- 1 teaspoon of rose water
- 1/2 teaspoon of lemon juice
- 1/4 teaspoon of tartar cream
- 3/4 cup of confectioners' sugar

Cooking Directions

1. Pre-heat your oven to 200 degrees Fahrenheit
2. Take 2 baking sheets and line them up with parchment paper
3. Take a large bowl and mix chickpea water, rose water, tartar cream and lemon juice
4. Beat the mixture with an electric mixture for about 10-30 minutes until you get a nice even texture
5. Increase the speed to high and gradually add the confectioners' sugar until meringue starts to hold stiff peaks, this should take about 10 minutes of blending
6. Pipe up small mounds of the mixture onto your baking sheets
7. Bake for 1 and a 1/2 to 2 hours, making sure to rotate the sheet halfway through
8. Once they are completely dry and firm, allow them to cool and serve!

Nutritional Values

- Calories: 12
- Fats: 0g
- Carbs: 2.4g
- Protein: 0g

24 Fancy Coconut Date Bars for A Lovely Evening

Serving: 4
Prep Time: 10 minutes
Cook Time: 30 minutes

- 1/3 cup of slivered almonds
- 1/2 a cup of flaked coconut
- 12 pieces of pitted dates
- 1/4 cup of cashews
- 1 teaspoon of coconut oil

Cooking Directions

1. Take a food processor and add the almonds then blend them
2. Add dates and pulse until mixed well
3. Add coconut oil and cashews until the mix is thick and sticks together
4. Transfer the mixture to a wax paper and form nice squares
5. Fold up the sides of the wax paper over top the squares
6. Chill for at least 30 minutes and serve
7. Enjoy!

Nutritional Values

- Calories: 165
- Fats: 2g
- Carbs: 39g
- Protein: 1g

25 Vegan Coconut Whipped Cream

Serving: 6
Prep Time: 8 hours 10 minutes
Cook Time: 0 minutes

Ingredients

- 1 can of unsweetened coconut milk
- 3 tablespoons of white sugar
- 1 teaspoon of pure vanilla extract

Cooking Directions

1. Place the can of coconut milk in your fridge and allow it to chill for 8 hours
2. Make sure to chill a metal bowl and beats in your fridge for about 1 hour prior to preparing the whip
3. Open up your coconut milk can and scoop out the coconut cream solids into your metal bowl
4. Keep the liquids for later use
5. Beat the cream using a mixer on medium speed
6. Set the speed on HIGH and beat for 7-8 minutes until stiff peaks form
7. Add sugar, vanilla extract to the coconut cream and beat for 1 minute more
8. Give it a taste and add more sugar if needed
9. Enjoy with cakes or muffins!

Nutritional Values

- Calories: 13
- Fats: 0g

- Carbs: 2.4g
- Protein: 0g

26 Salty Peanut Butter Cookies

Serving: 9
Prep Time: 15 minutes
Cook Time: 0 minutes

Ingredients

- 1 cup of raw almonds
- 1/2 a cup of peanut butter (creamy and unsalted)
- 1 and 1/2 cups of pitted Mejdool dates
- 1 and a 1/4 teaspoon of vanilla extract
- Sea salt as needed

Cooking Directions

1. Take a food processor and add almonds, peanut butter, vanilla, dates and blend the whole mixture until a dough like texture comes (should take a few minutes)
2. Add some more peanut butter if you want a stickier dough
3. Form balls using the dough and press down using a fork to create a cross pattern
4. Sprinkle salt generously
5. Serve immediately or allow it to chill for crunchiness

Nutritional Values

- Calories: 354
- Fat: 17g
- Carbohydrates: 27g
- Protein: 20g

27   Snowy Salad Bowl

Serving: 3
Prep Time: 75 minutes
Cook Time: 0 minutes

Ingredients

- 1 cup of white sugar
- 2 cups of water
- 1 can of 20-ounce frozen orange juice concentrate (thawed)
- 1 can of 20-ounce frozen lemonade concentrated (thawed)
- 4 sliced up bananas
- 1 can of crushed pineapple (with juice)
- 1 pack of strawberries (thawed)

Cooking Directions

1. Take a bowl and add water and sugar
2. Dissolve the sugar and add orange juice, bananas, lemonade, crushed pineapples (alongside the juice), strawberries and give it a nice mix
3. Pour the mixture into a 9x13 inch glass pan and allow it to chill
4. Once ready to serve, let it sit for about 5 minutes at room temp and cut them out

Nutritional Values

- Calories: 350
- Fats: 1g
- Carbs: 89g
- Protein: 2.5g

28   Classic Poached Pears

Serving: 4
Prep Time: 3 minutes
Cook Time: 17 minutes

Ingredients

- 4 semi ripe pears
- 3 and a 1/2 cups of water
- 3 cups of granulated sugar
- Rind of 1 lemon
- Juice of 1 lemon
- 1 teaspoon of vanilla extract
- 2 cinnamon sticks
- 2 pieces of whole cloves
- 1 whole star anise

Cooking Directions

1. Peel your pears and keep them on the side
2. Take a pot and add vanilla extract, water, lemon juice, sugar, lemon rind, star anise, cinnamon sticks and cloves
3. Place it over medium heat and keep cooking until the sugar dissolves
4. Add your peas and lower down the heat to low
5. Allow it to simmer for 15-20 minutes
6. Once the pears are soft, transfer to a Tupperware with cooking liquid
7. Allow it to cool
8. Serve and enjoy!

Nutritional Values

- Calories: 745
- Fat: 4g
- Carbohydrates: 180g
- Protein: 7g

29 Pristine Pineapple Sherbet

Serving: 4
Prep Time: 20 minutes
Cook Time: 0 minutes

Ingredients

- 1 can of 8-ounce pineapple chunks
- 1/3 cup of orange marmalade
- 1/4 teaspoon of ground ginger
- 1/4 teaspoon of vanilla extract
- 1 can of 11-ounce orange sections
- 3 cups of pineapple, lemon, or lime sherbet

Cooking Directions

1. Drain the pineapple, making sure to reserve the juice
2. Take a medium sized bowl and add pineapple juice, ginger, vanilla and marmalade to the bowl
3. Add pineapple chunks, drained mandarin oranges as well
4. Toss well and coat everything
5. Free them for 15 minutes and allow them to chill
6. Spoon the sherbet into 4 chilled stemmed sherbet dishes
7. Top each of them with fruit mixture
8. Enjoy!

Nutritional Values

- Calories: 267
- Fat: 1g
- Carbohydrates: 70g
- Protein: 2g

Rough and Tough Fried Apples

Serving: 4
Prep Time: 10 minutes
Cook Time: 10 minutes

Ingredients

- 1/2 a cup of vegan butter
- 1 cup of white sugar
- 2 tablespoons of ground cinnamon
- 4 pieces of Granny Smith Apples, peeled, sliced and cored

Cooking Directions

1. Take a large sized skillet and place it over medium hat
2. Add the vegan butter and allow it to melt
3. Stir in cinnamon and sugar into the melted butter
4. Add the cut-up apples and cook them nicely for about 5-8 minutes until they break down
5. Enjoy!

Nutritional Values

- Calories: 345
- Fat: 22g
- Carbohydrates: 44g
- Protein: 2g

 **Mind Blowing Tofu Mocha Bars**

Serving: 3
Prep Time: 5 minutes
Cook Time: 10 minutes

Ingredients

- 12 ounces of silken tofu (make sure to not drain it)
- 2 tablespoons of safflower oil
- Just a pinch of salt
- 2 and a 1/2 cup of sugar
- 1 cup of cocoa powder
- 1/3 cup of instant coffee powder (decaf)
- 1 teaspoon of vanilla extract
- 1 cup of whole wheat flour

Cooking Directions

1. Pre-heat your oven to 325 degrees Fahrenheit
2. Take an electric mixer and blend tofu until a creamy texture is obtained
3. Add salt, oil, cocoa, sugar coffee and vanilla and blend it again
4. Once the sugar has dissolved, remove the mixture from your blender and whisk in flour
5. Pour the batter into a greased up 9x13 inch baking pan
6. Bake for about 25-30 minutes until the cake starts to pull away from the sides of the pan
7. The bar should give you a glossy finish, take them out and allow it to cool. Cut them using a clean (wet) knife and serve!

Nutritional Values

- Calories: 151
- Fats: 2g
- Carbs: 22g
- Protein: 2.4g

32 Fancy Chai Masala Brownies

Serving: 3
Prep Time: 10 minutes
Cook Time: 20 minutes

- 2 tablespoons of unsweetened cocoa powder
- 1/3 cup of unsweetened shredded coconut
- 1 cup of all-purpose flour
- 1 and 1/2 cups of white sugar
- 1/2 cup of unsweetened cocoa powder
- 1/2 a teaspoon of baking powder
- 1/2 a teaspoon of salt
- 1/2 a cup of strongly brewed masala chai (Spiced Tea)
- 1/2 a cup of canola oil
- 1/2 a teaspoon of vanilla extract

Cooking Directions

1. Pre-heat your oven to 350 degrees Fahrenheit
2. Take an 8x8 inch baking pan and grease it up with cooking spray
3. Dust it well with 2 tablespoons of cocoa powder
4. Transfer it to a blender and pulse to mince them up
5. Take a bowl and add flour, 1/4 cup of cocoa powder, sugar, salt and stir in your chai alongside canola oil and extract
6. Keep stirring until the whole mixture is moist
7. Fold in your coconut
8. Spread the batter across your prepped pan
9. Bake for about 20 minutes until the top no longer shows a shiny texture

10. Allow it to cool for 1 hour
11. Cut it up and enjoy!

Nutritional Values

- Calories: 256
- Fats: 15g
- Carbs: 37g
- Protein: 3g

33 Dreamy Coconut Cookies

Serving: 10-15
Prep Time: 10 minutes
Cook Time: 0 minutes

Ingredients

- 3/4 cup of coconut flour
- 2 cups of smooth cashew butter
- 3/4 a cup of pure maple syrup
- 1-2 tablespoon of sprinkles

Cooking Directions

1. Take a large sized baking tray and line it up with parchment paper
2. Take a large sized mixing bowl and add coconut flour
3. Add the cashew butter and maple syrup as well and mix the whole mixture until it is nice and combine
4. Stir the sprinkles
5. Add some more coconut flour if the batter is too thin
6. Alternatively, add some water if the batter is too thick
7. Form small balls using the batter and place them on your parchment paper
8. Press the balls into cookie shape
9. Allow them to chill for a while and serve!

Nutritional Values

- Calories: 113
- Fat: 2g
- Carbohydrates: 5g
- Protein: 18g

34 Tasty Thai Fried Bananas

Serving: 3
Prep Time: 10 minutes
Cook Time: 15 minutes

Ingredients

- 3/4 cup of white rice flour
- 1/4 cup of tapioca flour
- 3 tablespoons of white sugar
- 1 teaspoon of salt
- 1/2 a cup of shredded coconut
- 1 and a 1/2 cup of water
- 10 bananas
- 3 cups of vegetable oil

Cooking Directions

1. Take a medium sized bowl and add rice flour, sugar, tapioca, coconut and salt
2. Stir in water and a bit of lime (little by little) until you have a thick batter
3. Peel up your bananas and cut each of them lengthwise into 3-4 pieces
4. Take a deep-fryer and add oil to 375 degrees Fahrenheit
5. Coat your bananas in the batter and fry them in oil
6. Drain and serve!

Nutritional Values

- Calories: 135

- Fats: 5.1g
- Carbs: 24g
- Protein: 1.2g

35 Delicious Pumpkin Pie Pastries

Serving: 25
Prep Time: 10 minutes
Cook Time: 8 minutes

Ingredients

- 1/2 a pack of rolled up unbaked pie crust (Vegan Compliant)
- 1 tablespoon of melted Vegan butter
- 3 tablespoons of packed brown sugar
- 1 and a 1/2 teaspoons of pumpkin pie spice

Cooking Directions

1. Pre-heat your oven to a temperature of 400 degrees Fahrenheit
2. Unroll the pie crust according to the package directions following the microwavable method
3. Place it on a lightly floured surface
4. Brush up the pie crust with melted butter
5. Sprinkle with pie spice and brown sugar
6. Take a pizza cutter and cut up the dough into 1/2-inch squares
7. Take an ungreased large cookie sheet and transfer them to the sheet, making sure to leave some space between the pieces
8. Bake for about 8 minutes until they are golden brown
9. Serve and enjoy!

Nutritional Values

- Calories: 50
- Fat: 2g
- Carbohydrates: 5g
- Protein: 0g

36 Warm Oven Roasted Plums

Serving: 3
Prep Time: 10 minutes
Cook Time: 15 minutes

Ingredients

- 5 plums, pitted and halved
- 1/2 a cup of orange juice
- 2 tablespoons of packed brown sugar
- 1/2 a teaspoon of ground cinnamon
- 1/8 teaspoon of ground nutmeg
- 1/8 teaspoon of cumin
- 1/8 teaspoon of cardamom
- 1/4 cup of toasted and slivered almonds

Cooking Directions

1. Pre-heat your oven to 400 degrees Fahrenheit
2. Take a shallow baking dish and grease it with cooking spray
3. Add your plums to the pan with the cut side facing up
4. Take a bowl and whisk in orange juice, cinnamon, brown sugar, cumin, nutmeg, and cardamom
5. Drizzle the mixture over your plums
6. Bake for 20 minutes until the plums are hot and the sauce shows a bubbly texture
7. Top with some almonds and enjoy!

Nutritional Values

- Calories: 113

- Fats: 4g
- Carbs: 23g
- Protein: 3g

37 Crisp Cinnamon Spiced Apples

Serving: 2
Prep Time: 5 minutes
Cook Time: 10 minutes

Ingredients

- 2 cored granny smith apples
- 1 tablespoon of brown sugar
- 1/4 teaspoon of ground cinnamon

Cooking Directions

1. Core the apples well and fill them up each with a serving of cinnamon and brown sugar
2. Wrap the apples using a large piece of heavy foil (making sure to make a few extra twist to make a handle)
3. Place the apples in a coal of campfire (or BBQ) and allow them to cook for about 5-10 minutes
4. Gently unwrap the apples and serve!

Nutritional Values

- Calories: 112
- Fats: 0g
- Carbs: 30g
- Protein: 0.5g

38   Crunchy Coconut Muffins

Serving: 4
Prep Time: 10 minutes
Cook Time: 30 minutes

Ingredients

- 3 cups of coconut milk
- 1 tablespoon of water
- 1 and a 1/4 cup of white rice flour
- 2 cups of shredded and unsweetened coconut
- 1 teaspoon of salt
- 1 tablespoon of white sugar

Cooking Directions

1. Pre-heat your oven to 375 degrees Fahrenheit
2. Take mini muffin tins and spray with cooking spray
3. Take a bowl and add coconut milk and water
4. Stir in white rice flour, salt and shredded coconut
5. Spoon up the mixture into your prepped mini muffin cups and sprinkle sugar on top
6. Bake in your pre-heated oven for 30 minutes until the tops are golden brown
7. Enjoy!

Nutritional Values

- Calories: 94
- Fats: 7g
- Carbs: 7g
- Protein: 2g

 # Energizing Peanut Butter Oatmeal Balls

Serving: 2
Prep Time: 20 minutes
Cook Time: 0 minutes

Ingredients

- 1 and 1/2 cups of dry oatmeal
- 2/3 cup of toasted coconut flakes
- 1/2 a cup of peanut butter
- 1/2 cup of ground flax seeds
- 1/2 a cup of semi-sweet dark chocolate chips
- 1/3 cup of agave nectar
- 1 tablespoon of chia seeds
- 1 teaspoon of vanilla extracts

Cooking Directions

1. Take a medium sized bowl and add all the listed ingredients
2. Mix them well
3. Cover it up and allow it to chill for a while
4. Once done, roll the mixture into 1-inch balls
5. It should make about 20-25 balls
6. Serve and enjoy!

Nutritional Values

- Calories: 135
- Fat: 10g
- Carbohydrates: 5g
- Protein: 11g

40   Vegan Snickerdoodle Balls

Serving: 4
Prep Time: 10 minutes
Cook Time: 10 minutes

Ingredients

- 1 and a 1/2 cup of whole wheat flour
- 1 cup of white sugar
- 1/2 a teaspoon of baking soda
- 1/2 a teaspoon of salt
- 1/2 a cup of vegetable oil
- 4 ounces applesauce
- 1 tablespoon of vanilla flavored almond milk
- 1 tablespoon of vanilla extract
- 1/2 a cup of cinnamon sugar

Cooking Directions

1. Pre-heat your oven to 375 degrees Fahrenheit
2. Take a bowl and add flour, baking soda, sugar, salt, and mix well
3. Take a large sized bowl and add vegetable oil, almond milk, apple sauce and vanilla extract
4. Add flour mix to this bowl and stir until well incorporated
5. Divide the dough into 14 portions and roll them up in balls
6. Spread cinnamon sugar into the wide and shallow bowl
7. Roll up the balls in the cinnamon sugar mix and arrange them on a baking sheet

8. Bake for 10 minutes in your oven until they show a nice golden brown texture
9. Enjoy!

Nutritional Values

- Calories: 188
- Fats: 8g
- Carbs: 23g
- Protein: 2g

41 Very Berry Bean Balls

Serving: 30
Prep Time: 10 minutes
Cook Time: 0 minutes

Ingredients

- 1 cup of dates
- 1 cup of dried berries and cherries
- 1/2 a cup of ground almonds
- 2 tablespoon of cocoa
- 2 tablespoon of runny agave nectar
- 3 and a 3/4 cup of black beans
- 1 small orange zest

As toppings:

- Cocoa
- Coconut
- Toasted Pistachios

Cooking Directions

1. Take a food processor and add dates, ground almonds, cocoa, honey, cherries, black beans, orange zest
2. Process the food well until they are finely chopped up
3. Use your hand to roll the mixture into balls
4. Garnish the balls with toasted cocoa, pistachios or coconut
5. Serve or store in fridge

Nutritional Values

- Calories: 325
- Fat: 14g
- Carbohydrates: 94g
- Protein: 8g

42   Silky Smooth Chocolate Pie

Serving: 16
Prep Time: 90 minutes
Cook Time: 0 minute

Ingredients

- 8 ounces of Dark Chocolate
- 1/4 cup of extra virgin olive oil
- 2 ripe Avocados
- 1 and 1/2 cups of coconut sugar
- 2 cups of cocoa powder
- 1 cup of heavy cream
- 1 tablespoon of vanilla
- 1/2 a teaspoon of espresso powder
- Just a pinch of salt

Cooking Directions

1. The first step here is to take a pan and toss in the dark chocolate and olive oil at medium heat
2. Once done, let the chocolate cool at room temperature
3. Then scoop out some avocado and place it in a mixing bowl
4. Add the chocolate coconut mixture to the bowl alongside cocoa powder and sugar
5. Whip up the mixture on medium speed using a mixer for about 2-3 minutes
6. Toss in the extract, cream, salt and espresso and whip it again on medium high to high speed for approximately 5 minutes until fluffy

7. Divide the batter into pie crust portions and chill them for a few hours
8. Serve with whipped cream!

<u>Nutritional Values</u>

- Calories: 73
- Fat: 5g
- Carbohydrates: 12g
- Protein: 1g

43 Beautifully Glazed Maple Candy

Serving: 4
Prep Time: 10 minutes
Cook Time: 10 minutes

Ingredients

- 3 cups of maple syrup
- 1 cup of chopped up walnuts

Cooking Directions

1. Take a large sized heavy bottomed saucepan and bring your maple syrup to a boil over medium high heat
2. Make sure to keep stirring it from time to time and keep boiling it until the temperature reaches 235 degrees Fahrenheit
3. Remove the heat and let it cool down for 10 minutes at 175 degrees Fahrenheit
4. Stir the mixture rapidly, then for 5 minutes use a wooden spoon until the color starts to turn lighter and the mixture starts to thicken
5. Stir in some chopped up nuts
6. Pour the mixture into molds and let it cool
7. Once cooled, unmold the candy and start gobbling up!

Nutritional Values

- Calories: 125
- Fat: 2.2g
- Carbohydrates: 24g
- Protein: 1g

Pumpkin Butter Cups

Serving: 5
Prep Time: 135 minutes
Cook Time: 0 minute

For Filing

- 1 cup of organic pumpkin puree
- 1/2 a cup of homemade almond butter
- 2 tablespoons of organic maple syrup
- 4 tablespoons of organic coconut oil
- 1/4 teaspoon of organic ground nutmeg
- 1/4 teaspoon of organic ground ginger
- 1 teaspoon of organic ground cinnamon
- 1/8 teaspoon of organic ground clove
- 2 teaspoons of organic vanilla extract

For Topping

- 1 cup of organic raw cacao powder
- 4 tablespoons of organic maple syrup
- 1 cup of organic coconut oil

Cooking Directions

1. Take a medium sized bowl and add all of the ingredients listed under pumpkin filling
2. Mix them well until you have a creamy mixture
3. Take another bowl and add the remaining ingredients and mix until creamy and smooth

4. Take a muffin cup and fill it up with 1/3 of the chocolate topping
5. Chill it in your freezer for about 15 minutes
6. Add another 1/3 of the pumpkin filling this time and layer another chocolate layer on top
7. Chill for 2 hours
8. Serve and enjoy!

Nutritional Values

- Calories: 105
- Fat: 12g
- Carbohydrates: 4g
- Protein: 2.9g

45   **Thin Carrot Crisps**

Serving: 4
Prep Time: 50 minutes
Cook Time: 10 minutes

Ingredients

- 4 cups of carrots sliced paper thin
- 2 tablespoons of olive oil
- 2 teaspoons of ground cumin
- 1/2 a teaspoon of smoked paprika
- Pinch of salt

Cooking Directions

1. Pre-heat your oven to 215 degrees Fahrenheit
2. Slice up the carrots into paper thin coin shapes
3. Add the slices to a bowl and toss well with spices and oil
4. Mix and lay them out on a baking sheet lined up with parchment paper
5. Sprinkle salt
6. Bake for 8-10 minutes and enjoy!

Nutritional Values

- Calories: 245
- Fat: 0g
- Carbohydrates: 2g
- Protein: 0g

 # Magnificent Mango and Chia Pudding

Serving: 4
Prep Time: 10 minutes
Cook Time: 60 minutes

Ingredients

- 1 whole mango completely peeled up and pureed
- 1 and 1/2 cups of 250ml coconut milk
- 3 tablespoons of chia seed

Cooking Directions

1. Take a bowl and add the listed ingredients
2. Give it a nice stir and allow them to chill for an hour
3. Serve!

Nutritional Values

- Calories: 135
- Fat: 24g
- Carbohydrates: 15g
- Protein: 23g

47   Sassy Chocolate Mousse

Serving: 4
Prep Time: 10 minutes
Cook Time: 0 minute

Ingredients

- Coconut cream scraped from the upper side of 2 pieces of 13.5-ounce chilled cans of full fat coconut milk
- 5s tablespoon of cocoa
- 3 tablespoons of Agave Nectar
- 1 teaspoon of vanilla extract

Cooking Directions

1. Take a large bowl and scoop out the thick coconut cream from the can to the bowl
2. Add nectar, vanilla extract and cocoa to the bowl
3. Beat it well using an electric mixer, starting from low and going to medium until a foamy texture appears
4. Divide the mix evenly amongst ramekins and chill to your desired level of cold
5. Enjoy!

Nutritional Values

- Calories: 134
- Fat: 3.8g
- Carbohydrates: 16g
- Protein: 3.8g

48 Tender Heirloom Carrots

Serving: 3-4
Prep Time: 10 minutes
Cook Time: 45 minutes

Ingredients

- 2 bunches of fine heirloom carrots
- 1 tablespoon of fresh thyme leaves
- 1/2 a tablespoon of coconut oil
- 1 tablespoon of maple syrup
- 1/8 cup of fresh squeeze orange juices
- 1/8 teaspoon of sea salt
- Salt as needed

Cooking Directions

1. Pre-heat your oven to 350 degrees Fahrenheit
2. Wash your carrots well and discard any green pieces
3. Take a small sized mixing bowl and add coconut oil, maple syrup, orange juice and a bit of salt
4. Pour the mixture over your carrots and spread on a large sized baking sheet
5. Sprinkle a bit of thyme and roast for 45 minutes
6. Sprinkle a generous amount of salt and a bit of thyme as garnish
7. Enjoy!

Nutritional Values

- Calories: 83

- Fat: 2g
- Carbohydrates: 12g
- Protein: 1g

49 Fresh and Healthy Cucumber Avocado Bowl

Serving: 4
Prep Time: 45 minutes
Cook Time: 0 minute

Ingredients

- 3 medium sized cubed cucumbers
- 2 cubed avocados
- 4 tablespoons of chopped up fresh cilantro
- 1 minced garlic clove
- 2 tablespoon of minced green onion
- 1/4 teaspoon of salt
- Black pepper as needed
- 1/4 large lemon
- 1 lime

Cooking Directions

1. Take a large sized bowl and add cucumbers, cilantro and cucumbers
2. Stir in the onion, garlic, pepper and salt
3. Squeeze lemon and lime over the top and toss well
4. Let it chill in your fridge for 30 minutes
5. Serve and have fun!

Nutritional Values

- Calories: 175
- Fat: 14g
- Carbohydrates: 14g
- Protein: 3.1g

50   Zesty Sweet Potatoes

Prep Time: 10 minutes
Cooking Time: 30 minutes
Serving: 7

Ingredients

- 1/4 teaspoon of pepper
- Vegetable cooking spray
- 1 tablespoon of finely chopped fresh parsley
- 1 teaspoon of grated orange rind
- 2 minced garlic cloves

Cooking Instructions

1. Take a large sized bowl and add the first 4 ingredients
2. Toss everything well
3. Take a large baking sheet and grease it with cooking spray
4. Arrange your sweet potato slices in a single layer
5. Pre-heat your oven to a temperature of 400 degrees Fahrenheit and let it cook for about 30 minutes
6. Make sure to turn the potatoes after 15 minutes
7. Take a small bowl and add parsley, garlic and orange rind
8. Mix them well
9. Sprinkle the parsley all over the baked potato slices and serve!

Nutritional Values

- Calories: 175
- Fat: 25g
- Carbohydrates: 366g
- Protein: 25g

Conclusion

I would like to thank you again for purchasing the book and taking the time for trying out the recipes.

I do hope that this book has been helpful, and you found the information contained within the recipes useful!

Keep in mind that you are not only limited to the recipes provided in this book! Just go ahead and keep on exploring you will find a gold mine of amazing vegan desserts out there to try out.

If you received value from this book, then I'd like to ask you for a favor. Would you be kind enough to leave a review for this book on Amazon?

Click Here to Leave a Review on Amazon!

https://www.amazon.com/review/create-review/ref=dpx_acr_wr_link?asin=B078QM3XRF#

I want to help as many people as I can with this book; more reviews will help me to accomplish that!

FREE DOWNLOAD

THE QUICKEST WAY TO GET IN SHAPE AS A VEGAN...

Sign up for Clark Johnson's New Releases mailing list and get a free copy of the latest book: *Vegan Warrior*

Click here to get started:

http://bit.ly/VeganWarriorBook

Printed in Great Britain
by Amazon